The Art of Loving

Chiara Lubich

The Art of Loving

Preface by
Cardinal Francis George

Introduction by
Amy J. Uelmen

New City Press
Hyde Park, New York

Published in the United States by New City Press
202 Comforter Blvd., Hyde Park, NY 12538
www.newcitypress.com
©2010 New City Press (English translation)

Translated by Eugene Selzer from the original Italian
L'arte di amare
©2005 Città Nuova Editrice, Rome, Italy

Cover design by Durva Correia

Biblical citations are taken from the New Revised Standard Version
©1989 Division of Christian Education of the National Council of the
Churches of Christ in the United States of America.
Library of Congress Cataloging-in-Publication Data

Lubich, Chiara, 1920-2008.
 [Arte di amare. English]
 The art of loving / Chiara Lubich ; preface by Francis George ;
introduction by Amy J. Uelmen ; [translated by Eugene Selzer
from the original Italian].
 p. cm.
 Includes bibliographical references.
 ISBN 978-1-56548-335-4 (pbk. : alk. paper) 1. Love—Religious
aspects—Catholic Church. 2. Christian life—Catholic authors.
3. Focolare Movement. I. Title.
 BV4639.L77313 2010
 241'.4—dc22   2010002958

3rd printing: July 2017

Printed in the United States of America

Contents

Be the First to Love

Love as You Love Yourself

"Make Yourself One"

Loving Jesus in Everyone

Mutual Love

The Risen Lord in Our Midst

Preface

*T*he *Art of Loving* could be an ambiguous book title were it not immediately followed by the name of the author: Chiara Lubich. Chiara's long life was testimony to a way of loving that extends to everyone because it was so completely immersed in the love of God. It begins with people rather than principles, with relationships rather than rules. It is an art that transforms the artist.

Chiara quotes most often from the Gospel according to St. John. "God is love," St. John writes and we remember. Too often, however, we might forget just how unique that claim is among world religions. In many faiths, God does love the world and its creatures; but the belief that self-sacrifice is the inner dynamic of God's own life is proper to a religion that worships one God in three divine Persons.

Because God is self-giving, those made in his image and likeness are called beyond generosity, the sharing of things, to self-sacrifice, the sharing of one's life. A sign of such love is joy. A fruit of such love is unity. The way that is the Focolare Movement is marked by joy and unity, with God and with others.

The family is a school of love, where we learn to give to others, to put them before ourselves, to make room for all. Chiara's spirituality embraces the world and the God who freely created it and redeemed it so that we could be sanctified while sharing our lives in community. In the Focolare community and the Church that protects it, we come to know God by living with him and interacting with him regularly, habitually.

Pope Benedict XVI has made love the *leitmotiv* of his magisterium, linking love to ideas and principles that have sometimes been placed outside of it or even in opposition to it: eros, justice, economics and business, politics and government. If God is love, then in some sense the quality of free gift, of gratuity, must be intrinsic to every human action. Chiara Lubich knew this truth and lived it intensely.

Mothers are the first to teach the art of loving, and the Focolare is the work of Mary, Mother of God and our mother in God's family. This book is one more gift from the Focolare Movement to the Church and to the world; it celebrates the gift given everyone in Chiara Lubich. The book's simplicity can hide its depth, but spending time with it will help anyone acquire the art of loving.

Francis Cardinal George, O.M.I.
Archbishop of Chicago

Introduction

"So, can you bottle it?"

At a conference exploring resources to strengthen religious identity in youth, I had been chatting with a friend and sharing something about my own experience growing up with the Focolare spirituality and its ongoing activities and programs for youth formation. He responded, "So, can you bottle it?" Bottle it? I was a little taken aback. "Probably not," was my initial reaction. At the root of the Focolare spirituality is a charism, a gift from God. It seemed to me that any attempt to contain it or to reduce it to a formula not only would be futile, but would miss the point entirely.

In fact, much of Focolare founder Chiara Lubich's experience can be summed up in her courage and capacity *not* to "bottle it." The narrative of her life is thick with examples of total availability and receptivity to the creative plans God wanted to work in her and in the movement that was coming to life. Chiara said more than once, "The pen does not know what it will write ... the artist's brush does not know what it will paint. When God takes someone in hand to bring a new work into being, that person does not know what she will achieve; she is simply an instrument." How can we harness something that is out of our hands? No one ever sat down to map out the Movement's future. It emerged from life.

As Chiara and her friends rushed to the shelters in their heavily bombed northern Italian hometown of Trent, the circumstances of World War II brought the group of young women to ask themselves, "Is there an ideal that does not die, that no bomb can destroy, to which we can devote our lives?" "Yes, there is," they felt from within. "That ideal is God. We decided to make God the ideal of our lives." From the very beginning they felt that God was the protagonist of their unfolding adventure.

Almost by chance, they brought to the shelters a small volume of the gospels, a book Roman Catholics at the time rarely consulted outside of Mass. "Love your neighbor as yourself" (Mt 19:19), they read. And they felt pushed from within to put those words into practice. All around they found "neighbors" to love: the old lady unable to make it to safety, the five children shaking with fear, the homebound invalid who needed medicine, the hungry, the thirsty, the injured. "Give and it will be given to you" (Lk 6:38): "If we had only one egg in the house for all of us we offered it to the poor. And what do you know, in the morning a bag of eggs arrived!" If they did have a formula, it was the life of the gospel, put into practice moment by moment.

Almost by chance the first community house came into being. Since their homes had been destroyed, several of the young women gathered in a small apartment that came to be known as the "focolare" (which in Italian means "hearth") because of the warm atmosphere of family and love that continues to be characteristic of these communities. In the constant effort to renew relationships of mutual love, they experienced the presence of the Risen Lord in their midst: "Where two or three are gathered in my name ..." (Mt 18:20). Only later did they realize that this "hearth" would come to express a new path for consecrated life in the Church.

This attitude of receptivity and availability is perhaps best expressed in how they gradually came to understand the specific aim of the Movement, to work for unity in the world. At a certain point during the war, as they huddled in a dark cellar, they read the prayer of Jesus to the Father, "That they may all be one" (Jn 17:21). Even though they were unsure of how to put it into practice, they intuited that this difficult passage was their *magna carta*. "We felt drawn to ask Jesus the favor of teaching us how to live unity," Chiara recounts. "Kneeling around the altar, we offered our lives to him so that through them, were it his wish, he could accomplish it."

The shape that the work for unity would take emerged over time. For example, in the early 1950s Chiara was asked whether the Movement would have something to do with ecumenical work in the service of unity with Christians of other denominations. She answered with a decisive "no," having envisioned at that point that the Movement's terrain of action was only the Roman Catholic Church. Only later, through contact with Lutherans and Anglicans in the early 1960s, did she realize how ecumenism would become integral to the Movement's identity. Similar stories describe the Movement's engagement with interreligious dialogue, or its spreading and growth throughout Italy, across Europe, even beyond the Iron Curtain, and to every continent.

While the Movement is known familiarly as "Focolare," the official name under which John XXIII approved it in 1962 is, "Work of Mary," a title that brings to mind another woman's capacity to be empty of herself, "Let it be done," in response to God's own plans. "So, can you bottle it?" Not any more than one can catch the subtle, gentle breath of the Spirit, and its creative work over time.

On second glance, the question, "Can you bottle it?" might also be understood as a desire to respond to the needs and concerns of our contemporary culture. In this sense the question deserves a more complex answer. If by "bottle" one means, "Can the spirituality be made available and easily accessible to a wide audience?", I believe that the answer is a resounding "yes."

In fact, everything about Chiara's life was geared toward making available and accessible to everyone a path to union with God and unity with each other. "This is the great attraction of modern times" — she wrote — "to penetrate to the highest contemplation while mingling with everyone, one person alongside others."

The various genres included in this book provide examples of how Chiara nourished the "highest contemplation" for the people of various cultural and social backgrounds who make up the Focolare Movement. Perhaps the most poignant is the genre of conference call messages. From 1980 through 2004, at first on a bi-weekly and then on a monthly basis, Chiara drafted brief messages, usually running about five to seven minutes, which she then shared with thousands of people throughout the world linked together in a global conference call. These served as an invitation to everyone who felt a particular affinity — all age groups and vocational paths within the Movement, children, youth, adults, consecrated people, married people, priests and religious, and, increasingly over the years, Christians of various denominations and faithful of other religious traditions — to plunge into one aspect or another of the Focolare spirituality in order to live it more fully, and then share with fellow travelers on the "Holy Journey" the results of this constantly renewed thrust toward sanctity in everyday life.

Similarly, she did not keep many parts of her diaries and meditative writings as only personal papers, but generously shared them with the community as a source of constant, thorough growing nourishment in the spirituality. Some of the excerpts in this book are also taken from Chiara's frequent spontaneous talks during which she answered questions so as to respond directly to the particular challenges that the community or other friends were facing.

If the question of "bottling" is taken to mean the possibility of the spirituality being made accessible to a wide audience, the answer can be seen in how Chiara herself envisioned that the Movement would lend increasing energies to this effort. For the first fifty or so years of the Movement's life, Chiara devoted relatively little time to public interviews or presentations of the Focolare's work and ideas. Instead, she focused her energy on helping members of its communities to grow and mature in living the Focolare spirituality in an authentic and radical way, and on strengthening the Movement's internal structures. Then in the early 1990s, Chiara herself and the Movement as a whole devoted increasing attention to the spirituality's doctrinal content and its cultural implications. This is perhaps best illustrated by the work of the Movement's interdisciplinary study center, the Abba School, and the 2008 inauguration of the Sophia University Institute, located near Florence, which now offers programs leading to master's and doctoral degrees in "Foundations and Perspectives of a Culture of Unity."

On this foundation, especially during the last decade of Chiara's life, the Movement turned toward the question of how its spiritual resources might help to renew various aspects of culture, from economics and politics to law and art, pedagogy and social work. Cultural work of this kind has required an increasing effort to develop a language that is accessible not only for the various disciplines but also for the different cultural and social contexts in which this project is embedded. Everything about this trajectory indicates that the delicate work of finding the language and conceptual frameworks to express what the Focolare spirituality has to offer will be an essential part of its focus and identity in this next stage of the Movement's development and growth.

"So, can you bottle it?" In a certain sense, this book can be read as an effort to do just that, for three reasons: first, its essential focus; second, its practical structure; and finally, the original context in which the texts were delivered.

First, this book focuses on an aspect of Chiara's charism that she herself considered a central and indispensable entry point to the entire Focolare spirituality. "Love is everything," she summed up in an interview. In some spiritualities love of neighbor flows as a direct consequence and expression of the primary love for God. While there is no doubt that for Chiara all love is rooted in God, the emphasis of her collective spirituality is slightly different. She described the connection in this way: "Our inner life is fed by our outer life. The more I enter into the soul of my brother or sister, the more I enter into God within me. The more I enter into God within me, the more

I enter into my brother or sister. God — myself — my brother or sister: it is all one world, all one kingdom" (*Essential Writings* 65).

Pope John Paul II picked up on the essential role of love in the Focolare spirituality during a 1984 visit to the Movement's headquarters outside of Rome. He spontaneously remarked: "Love is the inspiring spark for all that is done under the name Focolare, of all that you are, of all that you do in the world.... Love opens the way. I hope that thanks to you this way may be always more open for the Church." Confiding his concern that in various social and cultural contexts, hate and violence were being pursued in a programmatic way, he encouraged the Movement to pursue its "rich and beautiful" and even "programmatic" path of love. This book can be read as exactly that: a "program of love" that emerges from a spirituality centered on love.

Second, readers may also find that the book's practical structure gives unique insight into the Focolare spirituality itself. In that same encounter at the Movement's headquarters, John Paul II noted how the history of the C hurch had seen various expressions of the "radicalism of love," all of which were contained in "the supreme radicalism of Christ" — Francis of Assisi, Ignatius of Loyola, Charles de Foucauld, and so on. "There is also your radicalism of love, a radicalism that discovers the depths and simplicity of love and all that love requires in different situations and that tries to let this love win in every circumstance, in every difficulty."

The book's structure aims to provide the building blocks for constructing a life founded within "the depths of love" in a "radical" way. It does so through a set of deeply practical questions: What does it mean, really, to love "everyone" in a specific situation? After acknowledging the fact that small or big "enemies" might be a part of my everyday life, how can I take the step to "let love win" amidst these tensions? Amidst so many confusing definitions and attitudes in our world today, what exactly does it mean to love someone in a concrete and practical way? In a given situation, how can I come to recognize the ways in which my own interpretations, interests or preoccupations are blocking me from truly loving?

In fact, this book presents a relatively small slice of Chiara's efforts to make these points practical and accessible for people in a wide variety of settings and social contexts. For example, for elementary school children, the "Art of Loving" has been distilled into six points (I love everyone, I love my enemy, I love Jesus in the other, I share the other's joy or hurt, I am the first to love, We love one another). Each point makes up a face of what the children call the "Cube of Love." The children roll the cube, and commit themselves to living what comes out on top. With their families, or with other Focolare children, they share "experiences" of how love has changed their relationships and their perspective.

On several occasions, Chiara shared the basic points of the Art of Loving with Focolare members and other friends committed to living the Focolare spirituality as an integral part of their work in politics. Some have taped them to their computer screens or telephones, and eagerly look forward to opportunities for regular reflection on how these points may continue to serve as a powerful tool for transforming their approach to politics. Much of the Focolare's work in inter-religious dialogue is sustained by the effort to highlight in other religious traditions the values and resources that parallel a gospel-based Art of Loving. Profound bonds have been forged through the mutual exchange of insights that emerge from the effort to put these principles into practice.

Everything about this book speaks of a spirituality grounded in the effort to live the principles it explains. In thousands of social and cultural contexts throughout the world, that spirituality continues to nourish those everyday efforts to discover the meaning of "the depths of love" and to sustain the hope that love can "win." *The Art of Loving* offers an open invitation to practical reflection and practical commitment; in doing so it also captures the heart of the whole of the Focolare spirituality.

Finally, it is helpful to keep in mind the original context for many of these writings. As discussed above, many of the texts reflect Chiara's own work to "form" Focolare people to live a lifestyle of love in their everyday circumstances. For those less familiar with the Movement, some background on the characteristics of "formation" in Focolare communities might be useful.

First, it is helpful to keep in mind the extraordinary diversity of the people who Chiara engaged in constant conversation. She was aware that she was speaking to people from a variety of European settings, Western as well as Eastern, where, until the crumbling of the Berlin Wall, her writings and messages were passed on into underground communities and communicated in incredibly creative ways. In Asia and Africa, she knew that her words were nourishing people not only in countries with strong Christian roots like the Philippines and Korea, but also in settings where Christians constituted a tiny minority amid a larger Buddhist or Muslim population. As the message arrived to Latin America, the intended audience included both the impoverished and the powerful, as Focolare communities embrace people of all social backgrounds. The directness and simplicity in tone and language that mark Chiara's style allow her message to transcend cultural and linguistic differences, a striking expression of a charism at the service of the unity of all humanity, and of her personal love for her wide and varied audience.

Second, it is also helpful to situate these texts within the Focolare's intense focus on helping each other to discover what it means to "let love win" in the concrete circumstances and struggles of daily life. "Mutual love" is not simply one among many points or aspects. Mutual love is the very motor of the Movement and the entry point for an experience of Christ's presence that in turn truly illuminates what it means to love in any given circumstance. As the frontispiece to *The General Statutes of the Work of Mary* reads: "Mutual and constant love, which makes unity possible and brings the presence of Jesus among all" is the "norm of norms, the premise to every other rule."

I can illustrate both of these points with a small personal example. I have shared Chiara's insights on love with several colleagues at the Catholic law school where I work. Two in particular, who are Jewish, have found them helpful for their own spiritual journey, and for the work we share at the school. As a result, we have agreed to be on the lookout together for ways in which this "Art of Loving," as we each understand it within our own religious framework, might permeate our academic environment. For me, their faithfulness to this effort has been a profound source of inspiration and support in my own efforts to love.

Once, when I was feeling particularly down after another colleague had slighted me, one of these colleagues reminded me gently but firmly, "But you have to love your neighbor." He also offered a suggestion that ultimately helped heal the relationship. On another occasion, I was sitting next to my other Jewish colleague at a staff meeting in which a particularly difficult bureaucratic tangle was being discussed. He leaned over and whispered his general assessment of the situation: "We're not loving enough." This was the springboard for the two of us to propose to the administration together a creative solution for at least a part of the problem, and in a spirit of love and service to offer our help to implement the plan.

So these texts stand not only as an invitation to practical reflection and commitment but, where possible, also to living them *together*, so that love itself, the very presence of God among us, can illuminate what it means to love in a given situation.

In closing, a few suggestions on how to use this book. It can certainly be savored as a rich text for spiritual nourishment and personal edification. It could also be placed alongside any number of classics that reflect on the nature of love, such as C.S. Lewis's *The Four Loves*, or Erich Fromm's own *The Art of Loving*, to name just two. But if you really want to enter into the marrow of this work and to discover the true depth of its message, let these simple yet profound words challenge you and change the way you live and the way you love. Then share your discovery with others, who may very well want to join you in the adventure.

Amy J. Uelmen
Director, Institute on Religion, Law,
and Lawyer's Work, Fordham University

God
Is Love

"Beloved, let us love one another, because love is from God; everyone who loves is born of God and knows God."

(1 John 4:7–8)

Charity

Love. That is what God expects of every Christian, because in Christianity love is everything.

Saint Augustine, who taught about love, said very emphatically: "Christians are identified by love alone....

"Though they may all make the sign of the cross [a religious act], say 'Amen' and sing the 'Alleluia' [celebrating the liturgy, which is very important, but do nothing more ...], get baptized, go to church and construct basilicas, the fact remains that love alone identifies the children of God....

"Those who have charity are born of God and those who lack it are not born of God. That is the distinguishing factor.

"If you had everything else but were lacking this one thing, it would all count for nothing. If you have nothing else but this, you have fulfilled the law...."[1]

It Comes from Heaven

The gospel asks many things of us but there is one commandment that says it all.

According to Jesus it includes the "entire law and the prophets."

It is love, supernatural love, poured into our hearts by the Holy Spirit.

The Demands of Genuine Love

Charity is a most important virtue; in fact it is everything. It is good, therefore, to make an immediate effort to put it into practice. To do that we need to know what makes it special.

One writer says: "Loving is good, but knowing how to love is everything."[2] Yes, we must learn how because Christian love is an art and an art must be learned.

A great psychologist of our time said: "Our culture rarely seeks to learn the art of loving and, despite our desperate search for love, we end up considering everything else more important: success, prestige, money, power. We devote almost all of our energy to achieving these goals and make no effort to learn the *art of loving*."[3]

We find the real art of loving in Christ's gospel. Putting it into practice is an indispensable first step to setting off a revolution. It is a peaceful revolution, but one so forceful and radical that it will change everything. It affects not only the sphere of the spirit but the entire human sphere as well and renews every field it touches, whether cultural, philosophical, political, economic, academic or scientific. This revolution is the secret that enabled the first Christians to spread all over the entire known world.

The art of loving is challenging. It makes great demands....

It is an art that goes beyond the limited horizon of mere natural love, the kind of love we usually reserve for family and friends. But the love we are speaking of is directed toward everyone, good and bad, beautiful and ugly, fellow countryman or foreigner, co-religionist or not, one who shares my culture or one who does not, whether friend or adversary or enemy. We must love everyone as our Father in heaven does. He sends the sun and the rain on the good and on the bad.

This is a love which leads us to be the first to love, always, without waiting for the other to love us first. That is what Jesus Christ did in giving his life for us when we were still "bad" and unloving.

It is a love that makes us consider the other person as ourselves, that makes us see our very own selves in the other person. In the words of Gandhi: "You and I are but one. I cannot injure you without harming myself."[4]

It is a love not made up only of words or feelings; it is practical. It requires that we "make ourselves one" with others, that "we live the others" in a certain way, that we share their sufferings, their joys, in order to understand them, to serve and help them in an effective, practical way. It is a matter of weeping with those who weep, rejoicing with those who rejoice.

This art means that we love Jesus in the other person.

Our brothers and sisters are loved because we see Christ, who for us is God, in each one. We know that we will be saved only on the basis of this love. The majestic description of the universal judgment to be made by Jesus expresses it: to the virtuous he will say that all the good done to their brothers and sisters, and even what may have been evil, he takes as done to himself: "You did it to me" (Mt 25:40).

When several persons together practice this art of loving it leads to mutual love: in the family, at work, in groups, in society. Mutual love is the pearl of the gospel. It is the new commandment of Jesus. It builds unity.

These characteristics of true love as found in the gospel are what make it special.

Love Everyone

"But I say to you, Love your enemies and pray for those who persecute you, so that you may be children of your Father in heaven; for he makes his sun rise on the evil and on the good, and sends rain on the righteous and on the unrighteous."

(Matthew 5:44–45)

The First Characteristic of Love

The first characteristic of Christian love is that it reaches out *"to all."*

This way of loving requires that we love everyone, as God does, without distinction. We do not choose between who is nice or unpleasant, old or young, country- man or foreigner, black, white or yellow, European or American, African or Asian, Christian or Jew, Muslim or Hindu....

In today's terminology we could say that this kind of love avoids every form of discrimination.

Divine Love and Human Love

Supernatural love is essentially a participation in the very love of God, which is God himself. It differs infinitely from human love. The main difference is that human love makes distinctions; it is partial, loves certain friends, or only members of one's own family, or only the sophisticated or the rich or the beautiful or the respectable and does not love the rest, or at least not in the same way.

Divine love, instead, loves everyone. It is universal.

One Human Family

"Before all else, the soul must always fix its gaze on the one Father of many children. Then it must see all as children of the same Father. In mind and in heart we must always go beyond the bounds imposed on us by human life alone and create the habit of constantly opening ourselves to the reality of being one human family in one Father: God."

The note continues:

"Jesus, our model, taught us two things alone, and which are one: to be children of only one Father and to be brothers and sisters to each other."

Opening the Heart

We must break through all the barriers and open our hearts to the one human family, so we can say: I live for the one human family!

Since we are all brothers and sisters, we must love all. We must love everyone. This may seem like a very small thing, but it is revolutionary!

Everyone Is a Candidate for Unity

Universal brotherhood frees us from slavery, from being slaves to the divisions between rich and poor, between the generations, between parents and children, between black and white, between races and nationalities. We have been enslaved, we criticize one another, we have placed obstacles and barriers between us.

No, we must break all the chains of slavery and see others, without exception, as candidates for unity with God and unity among ourselves.

Banish Judgment

As Christians we must be committed to the *ut omnes** and then, first of all, we must renew our conviction that everyone is called to unity, because God loves everyone.

There are no excuses like: "So and so will never understand"; "that one is too young to understand"; "he is my relative and I know him well, he is attached to earthly things"; "she believes in spiritualism"; "he is of a different faith"; "she is too old to change."

No. Banish all such judgments. God loves all. He welcomes all.

---

* In fulfillment of what Jesus asks his Father at the Last Supper: *Ut omnes unum sint, sicut tu Pater in me et ego in te* ("That all may be one, as you, Father, are in me and I in you," Jn 17:21).

Who Is My Neighbor?

We must love everyone. We begin by loving our neighbor.

But who is our neighbor? We know who it is; we need not look far. It is the brother or sister who is near us at this present moment in life.

If we are to be Christians, we must love this neighbor right now, and not with some platonic or idealized love. It must be with a practical love, not in some abstract or distant way but in a concrete and effective way, right now.

The "Discovery"

During the Second World War when I and my companions went down into the air raid shelters, we would read the gospel. We read: "Love your neighbor as yourself" (Mt 19:19). My neighbor. Where is my neighbor?

There beside us. In that old lady barely able to drag herself each time to the shelter. We must love her as ourselves; we must help her each time, then, and support her.

The neighbor was there in those five frightened children alongside their mother. We must take them in our arms and help them home.

The neighbor was there in that sick person confined to home, unable to go to the shelter, but in need of care. We must go there and get him medicine.

One at a Time

We need to enlarge our heart to the measure of the heart of Jesus. How much work that means! Yet this is the only thing necessary. When this is done, all is done. It means loving everyone we meet as God loves them. And since we live in time, we must love our neighbors one by one, without holding in our heart any left-over affection for the brother or sister met a moment before. It is the same Jesus, after all, whom we love in everyone. If anything left-over remains, it means that the preceding brother or sister was loved for our sake or for theirs ... not for Jesus. That is the problem.

Our most important task is to maintain the chastity of God and that is: to keep love in our hearts as Jesus loves. Hence, to be pure we need not deprive our heart and repress the love in it. We need to enlarge our heart to the measure of the heart of Jesus and love everyone. And as one sacred host, from among the millions of hosts on the earth, is enough to nourish us with God, so one brother or sister, the one whom God's will puts next to us, is enough to give us communion with humanity, which is the mystical Jesus.

To have communion with our brother or sister is the second commandment, the one that comes immediately after the love of God, and is the expression of it.

Without Limit

Let us love our brothers and sisters. This is a great opportunity for us. We must not overlook a single one in the course of the day.

Let us love those whom we are normally aware of because they are physically present beside us.

But let us also love those who at times escape our attention: for example, those we talk about or talk to, those whom we remember in our prayers; those whom we hear about through the newspaper or TV; those who write us or to whom we write; those whom we work for day after day....

Let us love the living as well as those who are no longer with us here on earth.

To Serve

To love means to serve. Jesus gave us the example. By his death on the cross he served all of humanity, past, present and future. He also served us when he washed our feet. He was God, yet he washed the feet of mere human beings so we might learn to do the same for our brothers and sisters.

No, not so we "might" learn, rather we *must* learn that Christianity means serving. Serving everyone. Seeing everyone as our master. If we are servants, then the other must be our master.

Serve, serve. Aspire to the greatness of the gospel, yes, but by being of service to others.

Be at their service. That can start a worldwide revolution. Christianity is no joke, it is a very serious matter. It is not some little bit of superficiality: a little compassion here, a little love and charity there.

Christianity is demanding. It is life lived in its fullness.

A Maternal Heart

Look at it this way. I should act toward any neighbor I may meet or happen to work for, as though I were his or her mother.

A mother is always tolerant, ever ready to help, always hopeful, ever making excuses for her child. She forgives everything, even if the child is a delinquent or a terrorist.

A mother's love is like the charity of Christ, of which Saint Paul speaks (see 1 Cor 13: 1-13).

If we have the heart of a mother, or more precisely, the heart of Mary, the mother par excellence, we will be ready to love others in every situation.

We will love everyone, not just the members of our own Church, but those of others as well. And not just Christians but also Muslims, Buddhists, Hindus, etc. We will love nonbelievers of good will. We will not exclude anyone on earth because Mary's motherhood is universal, just as redemption is universal.

Even Our Enemies

"Love your enemies" (Mt 5:44). This overturns our normal way of thinking and alters the very course of our life!

Let's face it. It includes *any enemy whatever ... and we all have enemies* of one kind or another.

Perhaps the woman in the apartment next door, who is so unpleasant and meddlesome, who always tries to avoid getting into the elevator with us....

Or in that relative who thirty years ago did some injury to our father, so we have had nothing to do with him....

Or the one in the desk behind us at school, whom we totally ignore since she got us in trouble with the teacher....

Or that girl who was once our friend but then started going around with someone else ...

Or that sales person who cheated us....

Then there are those politicians who think differently from us, so we label them enemies.

Some see the state as an enemy and deliberately practice violence toward those who represent it.

There are those, like always, who see the clergy as their enemy and hate the Church.

All these *are to be loved* along with an infinite number of others whom we call enemies.

So we must love them!

Is that hard? Too painful? Does just thinking about it keep us awake at night?

It does require courage. But it is not the end of the world. It just takes a little effort on our part, with God doing the other 99 percent. Soon our heart will be overflowing with joy.

For a New World

We must create a new world where people love one another.

That is what God wants. We must begin somewhere.

In terms of strategy, it is up to Christians to begin. Since they experience God's love, they should be able to show love even to their enemies.

Christians are especially qualified to overcome the difficulties involved in loving because they are already in possession of a powerful love. As children of God they participate in the very love of God, a God who is Love.

Within Everyone's Reach

It is not sufficient just to banish war. Peace demands that we eliminate the category of enemy and never use that label for anyone. We must love everyone.

Christ's disciples are capable of doing this.

There is some degree of love in the depths of every human heart, including those who have no religious faith. They may call it philanthropy, solidarity or nonviolence, but it is the same love and respect for neighbor that religion invites people of faith to practice.

The Christian Revolution

Universal love has great potential. Many people already have the experience that if we were only to live this kind of charity, real love, the love of God, it would incite a revolution all around us, beginning right in our midst. It would be a Christian revolution, like that set off by the first Christians in their day.

Heaven on Earth

Love your brothers and sisters, each one individually and all of them collectively. Love your neighbors one by one and respect every nationality as a group.

This creates a radical change of mentality and initiates a whole new way of life.

If everyone did this, we would have heaven on earth.

Like the Creator

Faith in God's love for every creature, a hallmark of Christians, is something we have found present also in many of our brothers and sisters of other religions, beginning with the Abrahamic faiths which affirm the unity of the human race, God's care for all humanity and the duty of every human being to imitate the creator in his overwhelming mercy toward all.

As a Muslim saying puts it: "God forgives one hundred times, but reserves his greatest mercy for those whose piety spares the least of his creatures."[5]

Then there is the boundless compassion for every living being which the Buddha taught to his disciples: "O monks, you must act for the well-being of all, for the happiness of all, with compassion for the world, for the well-being of humanity."[6]

So love everyone. It is a universal principle. It has been heard by people of every age and place under heaven.

Be the First to Love

"In this is love: not that we loved God, but that he loved us and sent his Son to be the atoning sacrifice for our sins."

(1 John 4:10)

Take the First Step

Another step in the art of loving is being the *first to love* by always taking the initiative, without waiting for the other one to go first. This can be a real challenge for us, testing the authenticity and purity of our love.

This way of loving puts us at some risk, but if we are to love like God and develop the capacity to love which God has placed in our hearts, we must love as he does. He does not wait for us to love him but has always in thousands of ways shown us that he is the first to love, regardless of our response.

We were created to be a gift to one another, so we are faithful to our true selves when we reach out to our brothers and sisters with a love that precedes any sign of love on their part.

In Imitation of God

Christians must love as God does, not waiting to be loved first, but being "the first" to love. Since we cannot do this toward God because he is always the first to love, we must do it toward our neighbor.

St. John, after saying that God has loved us, does not conclude — as we might logically expect — that if God has loved us we must love him in return, but says rather: "Beloved, since God loved us so much, we also ought to love one another" (1 Jn 4:11).

Only because charity is a participation in the *agape* of God are we able to go beyond the limits of natural love, by loving our enemies and laying down our life for our brothers and sisters.

That is why Christian love brings us into a new era. This is a radically new commandment, which introduces something really "new" into human history and ethics. "This love — writes Augustine — renews us and makes us new persons, heirs of the New Testament, who have a new song to sing."[7]

Toward the Least Lovable

The love of God has taken the initiative and loved us when we were anything but lovable (we were dead through sin).

This thought takes me back to the first days of our Movement when God kindled in our hearts the "spark" (as John Paul II called it) of our great Ideal.

Perhaps it was because in the wretchedness of the war and all the desolation around us there was no one else to take the initiative in loving us.

No. It was a special gift of God that enabled us to light the flame of love in many hearts and hope that it might blaze up in all. We did not look to see whether our neighbors were lovable so that we could love them. Instead, we gathered around us the poorest of the poor and readily recognized in them the countenance of Christ. They were the ones who most needed his mercy.

He Taught Us

Perhaps it was to teach us to be the "first to love" that in that time of war God did not immediately move us to reach out to all our brothers. Instead he directed us toward the needy, the poor, the sick, the imprisoned and the orphaned. It seems now as though he put blinders on us so that we would see him only in them, and most especially in them.

We directed ourselves to all the poor of the city.

When we got off work, my companions and I carried heavy suitcases and visited them in their hovels. They were Jesus. We thought that on judgment day, the Lord would show us that piece of donated clothing, that scarf, those gloves we deprived ourselves of, now adorned with precious pearls, as happened with the little cross that Saint Catherine gave to the poor.[8]

The Lord showed us that the poor were the ones we could be the "first to love" (see Lk 14:13-14).

Gratuitous Love

With human love people as a rule love because they are loved. That kind of love may be beautiful, but one is loving something of oneself in the other person. There is always something egoistic about human love. We love when self-interest motivates us to love.

Divine love, instead, is gratuitous. It loves first.

If we want to let the "new person" in us come alive (see Eph 4:23), if we want to enkindle in ourselves the flame of supernatural love, we must be the first to love.

In Love what Counts Is to Love

In love what counts is to love. This is what it is like here on earth. Love (I speak of supernatural love which does not exclude natural love) is both so simple and so complex. It demands that you do your part and awaits the other's.

If you try to live only for love, you will realize that here on earth it is worthwhile doing your part. You do not know whether the other part will ever come; and it is not necessary that it should. At times you will be disappointed, but you will never be discouraged if you convince yourself that in love what counts is to love.

The Pact of Mercy

The first focolare* had an important experience of applying the principle of being the "first to love."

In those first days it was not always easy for a group of girls to practice love with all its radical demands. We were much like everyone else, even though we were supported by a special gift of God for starting the Movement. In our relationships too, dust could settle and unity be weakened. This would happen, for example, when we noticed some defects and imperfections in the others and made judgments, causing the flow of mutual love to grow cold.

To deal with this situation we decided one day to make an agreement among ourselves. We called it the "pact of mercy."

We decided each morning to see every neighbor we encountered — in the focolare, at school or at work — with new eyes, not remembering

---

* The author refers to the beginning of her experience in 1944 when seemingly fortuitous but providential circumstances allowed her to live together with other young women in the city of Trent, Italy. From this community of life was born the first focolare house, a living picture of the family of Nazareth, living in the midst of the world, virgins and married people together, all dedicated, although in different ways, to God.

any faults or defects, but covering everything with love. It meant approaching everyone with a full amnesty, extending pardon to all.

This was a great task to set for ourselves, but it helped us to be always the first to love, in imitation of God's mercy, who forgives and forgets.

Daily Resolutions

Get up in the morning and simply say: "I will be the first to love everyone I meet during the day. I will love this one and that one, and always be the first, be the first, be the first."

Always set out to be the first to love. What a marvelous way to live!

Set the tone, get the graces circulating, because when we love we invite the illumination of the Holy Spirit. Jesus says: "Those who love me.... I will love them and reveal myself to them" (Jn 14:21). Loving our neighbor means loving Jesus who always manifests himself and fills us with his light.

Many graces will rain down, leaving us tired at the end of the day but happy.

Love as You Love Yourself

"Love your neighbor as yourself."

(Matthew 19:19)

The "Golden Rule"

Another well-known characteristic of love is found in all the holy books. If this one thing alone were practiced, it would be sufficient to make the whole world a great family: *love as you love yourself,* do to others what you would want done to you, do not do to others what you would not want done to you.

This is the so-called "Golden Rule," which Gandhi expressed so well when he said: "You and I are but one. I cannot injure you without harming myself."[9] The gospel puts it this way: "Do to others as you would have them do to you" (Lk 6:31). The Muslim tradition says: "None of you are true believers if you do not desire for your brother what you desire for yourself."

This is the basis for a principle which, if applied, would be the greatest inducement to harmony among all kinds of people, between families and entire societies. Think what the world would be if not only individuals, but whole races and nationalities practiced the "Golden Rule" in this form: "Love the other's country as you love your own...."

A Law Written on Every Heart

"Do to others as you would have them do to you."

Let us love every neighbor we meet during the day like this.

Let us imagine we are in others' situations, treating them as we would want to be treated in their place.

The voice of God within us will suggest how to express the love appropriate to every situation.

Are they hungry? I myself am hungry, let us think. And we give them something to eat.

Are they being unjustly treated? So am I.

Are they in darkness and doubt? I am too. And we speak words of comfort and share their suffering; we do not rest until they find light and relief. We would want to be treated like this.

Do they have a disability? I will love them till I can feel in my own heart and body the same infirmity. Love will suggest to me how I can help them feel equal to others, indeed that they have an extra grace, because as Christians we know the value of suffering.

Let us do that for everyone without discrimination.

For All People of Good Will

We know that the "Golden Rule" in its various formulations is at the basis of practically every major religion in the world . It is truly a golden norm prescribing that we act toward others as we would want them to act toward us.

That is what it means to be Christian and Christians naturally speak that way.

But I believe this principle is not just for Christians, or for the various religions; it is for all men and women of good will, because it is based on reason. It is sound, just and universal.

Over and Above Nature

"Love your neighbor as yourself" (Mt 19:19). This puts us in a constant tension, because by nature we love ourselves.

The daily news often reports disasters, earthquakes and storms which leave many victims injured or homeless.

It is one thing to be among the victims, but it is quite a different thing when we are not.

Even when we manage to offer some aid or relief, we are not in their situation.

But tomorrow it will be the reverse: I will be on my deathbed (if there is a bed for me!) while others are out in the sun enjoying themselves.

"Love your neighbor as yourself." What Jesus commanded us is beyond our nature.

The *gift* he gave us, as he told the Samaritan woman, is not a human one.

But if we have within us that charity which by nature is divine, we can make real contact with the sufferings, concerns and joys of our neighbor.

With *this* love, a Christian love, we can truly comfort our neighbors. Tomorrow I may need their comfort. In this way we can truly begin to *live*, otherwise human life will be very harsh and arduous and at times almost impossible to bear.

You and Your Neighbor, Both Members of Christ

Every Word of God contains both the minimum and the maximum that he can ask of you, so when you read, "Love your neighbor as yourself" (Mt 19:19), you have the law of fraternal love at it highest degree.

Your neighbor is another you, and you must love him or her bearing that in mind.

When neighbors cry, you must cry with them, and when they laugh, laugh with them. If they lack knowledge, be ignorant with them. If they have lost a parent, make their suffering your own.

You and they are members of Christ and if one or the other is suffering, it is the same for you.

What has value for you is *God* who is both their Father and yours.

Do not seek to be excused from loving. Your neighbors are those who pass next to you, be they rich or poor, beautiful or not, brilliant or not, holy or sinful, a fellow citizen or a foreigner, a priest or layperson, whoever.

Try to love whoever appears to you in the present moment of your life. You will discover within yourself an energy and strength you did not know you had. It will add flavor to your life, and you will find answers to your thousand questions why.

Love Creates Equality

If we remain indifferent or withdrawn in the face of our neighbor's needs, whether they be on the material plane or on the spiritual, we cannot say we love our neighbor as ourselves. We cannot say we love as Jesus loved us.

If we take his love for us as our inspiration, then there can be no place for uneven treatment, inequality, partiality or indifference.

As Yourself

One of the things the Holy Spirit taught us through the charism of unity was this: that to understand the gospel passage — Love your neighbor as you love yourself — you must take it literally *without qualification*; in other words, not just as general advice. That word "as" means exactly that. So if I or someone else is in a certain situation, we must each experience it as though it were our own.

We realized that before this discovery our love for neighbor was far less than our love for ourselves. We were baptized Christians, we went to Mass daily, but we never thought to love the other as ourselves, even if there were times when our love went out to others. So we had to be converted and be concerned about the other *as* we were for ourselves.

So we did that with every neighbor we encountered and it set off a revolution.

Because when we start acting that way, people are struck by it; they are amazed and want to know what is going on. That gives us an opportunity to explain why we treat our neighbors in that way, serving and reaching out to them. Many of those who ask about this then feel that they want to begin to try living that way themselves.

Finally people who were indifferent to one another, and that generally includes all of us, even

Christians, begin to wake up; they take an interest in one another, begin to love one another and form community. We arrive then at the picture of a church which is alive, really living out that one passage of the gospel: "Love your neighbor as yourself," because, as St. Paul says, "For the whole law is summed up in a single commandment, 'You shall love your neighbor *as* yourself'" (Gal 5:14).

"Make Yourself One"

"I have become all things to all."
(1 Corinthians 9:22)

True Love

There is one aspect of the art of loving which teaches us how to put true love for others into practice. It is this simple formula, three little words: *make yourself one.*

Making yourself one with others means making their thoughts and problems your own, sharing their joys and sufferings.

God's Own Chosen Way

"To the weak I became weak. I have become all things to all people so that I might by any means save some" (1 Cor 9:22).

We really need to embrace this particular scripture verse. It tells us how to take part in accomplishing what Jesus asked of the Father: "May they all be one," which means "make yourself one with every neighbor."

Yes, this is the way, because it is the same way God himself chose to show us his love. He actually became human like us, to be crucified and forsaken. He reduced himself to our level. He truly became "weak with the weak."

Poor in Spirit

Make Yourself One.

These important words express *the* way of loving. What do these three little words mean and what do they require of us?

When we are filled with apprehension, with judgments or with thoughts ... of anything else, we are unable to enter into the heart of others to understand them, to accept them and share their sorrows. "Making yourself one" requires of us poverty of spirit. Only then is unity possible.

To whom do we look, then, to learn this grand art of being poor in spirit, an art which brings with it the Kingdom of God, — as the gospel says — a kingdom of spiritual love? We look to Jesus Forsaken. No one is poorer than he. After losing his disciples, and giving away his mother, he gives his life for us too and endures the terrifying feeling of being abandoned even by the Father.

Looking at him we understand how to do everything in the service of others out of love for them. We avail ourselves of the things of this world and — when necessary — even in some way the things of heaven in serving them. We realize how he felt abandoned by God, when love of neighbor may require (as it often does) that we leave God for God — in a manner of speaking. This happens, for example, when we must terminate our prayer and leave God in order to "make ourselves one" with someone in need. God is in that person inspiring us to empty ourselves completely so we can be open to the suffering of a neighbor. Looking to Jesus makes such renunciation possible.

"Making ourselves one" means accepting such renunciation.

"Making Ourselves One" in Everything

As we approach each neighbor we must know how to let go of everything we are doing that is beautiful, good and useful (even briefly if duty should call us to move on) in order to be ready to "make ourselves one" with that person in everything. We "make ourselves one" even to the point of being ready to die for him or her.

This is Christianity.

Dying to the Self

"Making ourselves one" embraces all aspects of life and is the fullest expression of love.

When we live that way we die to ourselves, to our own ego, and to every spiritual attachment.

We are able to attain that "nothingness of the self" to which the great spiritualities aspire. We reach that emptiness of love which is realized when we are really open to another.

So we must make room for them so that they can always find a place in our heart.

"Making ourselves one" means approaching everyone with willingness to learn, because we really have a lot to learn.

Letting Go of God — for God

"Making ourselves one" with others is not easy to do. It requires that we become completely empty, letting go of every idea from our minds, all feelings from our hearts, everything from our will, even silencing inspirations, losing God in ourselves for God present in others so that we can identify with them.

In the early days of the Movement when I was speaking with someone who wanted to confide in me, I realized I would eventually have to give some response and I tried for a long time to set aside my own ideas, so that she might be able to pour all that was in her heart. When I did this I was convinced that in the end the Holy Spirit would suggest to me exactly what I needed to say.

Why? Because I was "emptying myself" and was loving. So he manifested himself. I have experienced this thousands of times. If I had interrupted the conversation half-way through, I would have said the wrong thing. It would have been uninspired, mere "human" wisdom. Whereas when I let the other person unburden herself of all her anxieties and sorrows, I found the answer which resolved the situation and offered the most help.

Have a Heart of Flesh

We must be one with our neighbor not in some ideal way, but concretely, here and now and not just in some distant future.

Becoming one means feeling ourselves how the other feels. We deal with these feelings as though they were our own, since love makes them our own. Become the other. We do this out of love for ... Jesus in our brother or sister.

Discard this hard heart of *stone* and let your heart be one of flesh by loving others (see Ez 11:19).

"Pruning" Helps Love Grow

We must "make ourselves one" with every neighbor perfectly, by cutting away everything that stands in the way.

Many factors can deter this.

Sometimes we are distracted. At other times we have a desire to rush in with our own ideas or give advice at the wrong time. Sometimes we are poorly disposed to "make ourselves one" with our neighbors because we feel they do not appreciate our love. Or we may be hindered by our negative judgments about them. We might even be harboring an unconscious desire to win them over to our cause.

Sometimes we are incapable of "making ourselves one" because our heart is already preoccupied with its own problems, concerns and agendas.

How then can we "make ourselves one," and let the preoccupations, sorrows and anxieties of our neighbor find a way into our heart?

It is absolutely necessary to remove and eliminate everything that fills our mind and heart. Yes, we have to "cut away" in order to be more open, more disposed to love. We must "do some pruning" in order to love better.

Words of Substance

When we make ourselves perfectly one, Jesus gives an extraordinary authenticity to our words. They have a real validity, free of misleading embellishment, so that they pierce the heart of our neighbor like a sword and truly burn away all that is superfluous so that only the truth remains. Our neighbor can then grow in the truth, which is the same as growing in Jesus.

Hard Work

"Make yourself one," live the other, get totally involved.

"Make yourself one." Those are not empty words or pure sentiment. When Christians "make themselves one" they roll up their sleeves and get down to work. It means work, work, work, getting it done.

Jesus showed us what love is when he healed the sick, raised the dead, and washed the feet of the disciples. Move into action, get going; that is love.

Take upon Yourself
the Other's Burdens

It is important to understand love properly, in its most authentic sense.

We feel truly loved when someone makes us happy. So people will realize that our love is not genuine if, for example, we hold attitudes, discuss topics and spend our time on things of no interest to them.

The attitude that truly corresponds to the word "love" is *making ourselves one* by meeting the needs of others, taking on their troubles and sorrows. It means giving them food and drink, offering counsel and help.

What happens when we act that way?

When we become aware of the great problems in many areas of the third and fourth world which are in the grip of misery and short supply of housing, clothing, work, etc., we begin to understand that these people do not hope, for example, to create a new culture or raise their spirits by prayer. First we must do what we can to relieve their overwhelming burden of suffering. Then we start thinking of all the ways we can improve human life with education, comprehensive development, etc.

The same thing happens with individuals when we love them by "making ourselves one" with them. It completely lifts their burden and anxieties. They realize that we are taking upon ourselves what oppresses them and they feel liberated.

When they feel this relief they are freed of their preoccupations and are ready to embrace the message of love and peace that we bring.

They are attracted to the new, gospel-based life they see in us. Every heart yearns for this, because God desires it for all his children.

We Must "Be Love"

There are those who do things "for love." There are those who do things trying "to be Love." Those who do things "for love" may do them well, but, thinking they are doing great service for their neighbor, who is sick for instance, they may annoy them with their chatter, their advice and with their help. Such "charity" is burdensome and inappropriate.

They may gain merit, but the other is left with a burden. This is why it is necessary to "be Love."

Our destiny is like that of the planets: if they revolve, they are; if they do not, they are not. We *are*, in the sense that the life of God, not our life, lives in us, if we do not stop loving for one moment.

Love places us in God and God is Love.

But Love, which is God, is light and with the light we see whether our way of approaching and serving our brother or sister is according to the heart of God, as our brother or sister would wish it to be, as they would dream of it being, if they had beside them not us, but Jesus.

In Everything But Sin

How far must I go in "making myself one" with my neighbors, in loving and serving them in order to achieve eventual unity? Jesus himself gives us the answer. He made himself one with us by becoming man; he then experienced our weariness, our suffering, even to the point of death. He experienced everything that is part of being human, except sin.

We must do the same, and "make ourselves one" with whomever we encounter in the present moment of our lives. We must experience their cares, their sorrows, their joys, everything but sin.

Only then will this Christian manner of loving be blessed and productive. Many will respond to it. The circle of those who want God for their ideal will widen around each of us, like that of a stone cast into water.

The Risk of Speaking Out

To love it is necessary first "to make ourselves one" with our neighbors in everything but sin. That is fine. But it should not become a pretext for avoiding the risk of speaking out. We must be careful not to confuse true and false prudence, by getting stuck in a deplorable silence.

Jesus certainly made himself one with everyone, changing water into wine, multiplying bread, calming the tempest, curing the sick and raising the dead. But at the same time he spoke out. And how! It evoked both love and hate.

It will be the same for us, but that must not be an excuse for silence.

Let us listen carefully to the guiding voice within. We will find ever new possibilities for communicating our gift, whether convenient or inconvenient as St. Paul says (see 2 Tim 4:2).

The Gift of the Other

When we make ourselves one with others, they open up and reveal something of themselves. They disclose their identity. They express and share something of who they are as Jew, Muslim or Buddhist....

They enlighten us and surprise us with their own immense riches.

Believing and Enduring All Things

"Making ourselves one" involves all the qualities listed by St. Paul in his "hymn to charity" (see 1 Cor 13:1–13).

First of all, to "make ourselves one" we need to be forbearing, which means free of all impatience.

Making ourselves one certainly requires kindness.

Such an attitude is far removed from jealousy.

To make ourselves one we cannot be inflated, but must be empty of self.

We think only of the other and so there is no room for ambition or selfishness.

When we make ourselves one we are not quick-tempered. We must keep our calm. We do not rejoice over wrongdoing, because when we make ourselves one we are hoping instead that the other will triumph in goodness, justice and truth.

Making ourselves one is bearing, believing and enduring all things.

Even Suffering

We love our neighbors when we identify with their experience, and anticipate any needs they may have. That is what it means to love our neighbor.

But it involves even more.

If we look to Jesus, we can see that he loved his neighbors by relieving their hunger, curing them, forgiving them, etc. And he did not stop there. In order to love perfectly and completely he suffered and gave his life for them.

His action should provide some enlightenment for us. We should be able to infer from it that for us too, loving our neighbors cannot stop at "making ourselves one" with them. It involves something more. We call it suffering.

The life we live in this world certainly has its joys. It offers us some profound satisfactions as, for example, the advancement of the Kingdom of God. But there is no denying that it is also marked by suffering: illness, temptations, distress, torments, miseries, misunderstandings and unforseen misfortunes....

What meaning is there to all these sufferings? Why does God-Love permit them? We see in them the countenance of Jesus Forsaken, so we embrace them,* but often we do not ask ourselves

---

* Chiara Lubich has always seen in the cry of Jesus at

about the reason for such suffering. Since God makes all things work together for good, there must always be some precise purpose for every affliction. These things are intended by God or at least allowed by him for our purification and for the welfare of others, for their spiritual growth and advancement toward God.

Yes, there is always a reason.

---

the height of his passion ("My God, my God, why have you forsaken me?" Mk 15:34) the moment when he took upon himself all the sorrows of humanity and nearly personified them. He is the lonely, the tired, the dumb, the anguished, the one who failed.... Therefore she invites us to recognize his face in any physical or spiritual suffering, embrace it in acceptance (that is, take it upon ourselves) and continue to love.

Until Love Is Mutual

Making ourselves one. That is love.

Make yourself one with everyone you encounter during the day.

Make yourself one, so that the one who is loved may come to understand what love is and will want to love in turn.

This gives rise to mutual love, which is the distinguishing quality of Christians today just as it was in the days of Jesus' first disciples.

Mutual love, the commandment par excellence of Jesus, is the life of the Holy Trinity transplanted on earth.

Perfect mutual love is radical because it puts into practice the "as I have loved you" which is the measure of Jesus' love: in his abandonment he gave himself completely for us, losing — in some way — his very union with God.

Mutual love, when we practice it, accomplishes unity and generates Jesus in our midst.

It Is Jesus!

"Making ourselves one" sooner or later "wins the day."

What happens is that the others begin to love and make themselves one. They try to make themselves one with everyone, including us.

Then we are two who are "making ourselves one," truly loving each other as Jesus wants us to. He wants us to love even to the point of dying for one another. Not that when we love each other we expect to die tomorrow or the day after or next year. He wants us to die now, that is, to live as dead, dead to ourselves because we are alive to love.

When two souls meet and love each other this way, something truly extraordinary happens.

Just as when two elements are combined and form a third, which is not a mixture of the two but something new, so also when two people love each other in this way, each ready to die for the other, a third reality emerges. They are no longer the one or the other, or a mixture of the two, or a group of two or more: It is Jesus! Jesus! How marvelous!

"Where two or three are gathered together in my name — says Jesus — (which means in this love, in me), there am I in the midst of them." That means he is in them.

Loving Jesus in Everyone

"Truly I tell you, just as you did it to one of the least of these who are members of my family, you did it to me."

(Matthew 25:40)

"You Did It to Me"

Evangelical love means that we see *Jesus in our neighbor*, as he said in describing the last judgment: "For I was hungry and you gave me food, I was thirsty and you gave me something to drink.... Then the righteous will answer him, 'Lord, when was it that we saw you hungry and gave you food, or thirsty and gave you something to drink?...' Truly I tell you, just as you did it to one of the least of these who are members of my family, you did it to me" (Mt 25:35, 40).

Love like this requires that we see Jesus in every brother and sister and believe he is there because he considers done to him whatever good or evil we do to others.

An "Other Christ"

"You did it for me."

If Christ is somehow present in everyone, we cannot show any discrimination or prefer some people over others.

Human distinctions according to nationality, age, social condition, personal talent, wealth or whatever vanish into thin air. Christ is behind every person, he is in each one.

Every neighbor whose soul is filled with grace can be called an "other Christ." Even if grace is presently lacking, each one is at least potentially an "other Christ."

Clear Sight

Let your sight be clear so you can see there is one Father. Serve God in your neighbor. You have but one brother: Christ.

A clear eye sees everyone as "a Christ *in process*." We are ready to be of service to everyone … because we see Christ enter them and begin to grow there. See everyone as a new child of God; as Christ is born in them to grow, live and do good, so that he might die, rise and be glorified.…

We will find no peace until — by continuous faithful service — we see in our neighbor the spiritual features of Christ.

Therefore live Christ … by serving him in your neighbor where he is growing in age, wisdom and grace.…

This is how we will achieve the main goal of Jesus, his Ideal "that all may be one": when in every present moment we bring forth fruit in service of our neighbor.…

In Every Relationship: Charity

We must transform with charity the various contacts we have with our neighbors throughout the day.

From morning rising till nighttime retiring, every relationship with others must be one of charity. In church, at home, in the office, at school and on the street we must take every opportunity to practice charity.

Does our work involve teaching, instructing, guiding, feeding, clothing, caring for the family, serving our customers, carrying on business? Then we should do everything for Jesus in our neighbor, neglecting no one, always being the first to love.

It is a daylong effort, but worthwhile, because it is the way we move forward in the love of God.

Until Morning

We can love Jesus also in our family as we say "Good morning," and hopefully take time for morning prayer and breakfast.

We can love Jesus in our neighbors during the day, even from behind the school desk where we teach, at the store counter or at the bank window where we work.... We can love our neighbors by seeing Christ in them even when we are at home dusting or sweeping, washing dishes or out shopping.

We can love Jesus when we are writing a letter, making a phone call, going to a meeting or writing an article. We can love Jesus in our neighbor when we pray.

This wonderful opportunity is always there for us and we can be certain that he is continually saying to us: "You have done it for me."

Our Neighbor: A Goldmine

See the countenance of Jesus in every neighbor and love him there.

Realize that meeting a neighbor is like finding a goldmine where a golden nugget awaits us.

That is because we enrich ourselves every time we love our neighbor. "To everyone who has [love], more will be given" (see Mt 25:29).

St. Augustine was also convinced of that too. He says: "With love of neighbor, the poor are enriched; without love of neighbor the rich are impoverished."[10]

The Pearl

In our day "holiness should flourish in the religious congregations, as well as in our homes, schools, our streets, our offices and in parliament … ,"[11] because today we are much more aware that the laity too are called to holiness.

Can they not find union with God in the midst of the world, without needing to be isolated and sheltered behind walls with all those practices the spiritual life once required of us?

Now people are no longer in a protective environment; they are surrounded by other men and women, who were once to be kept at a distance.

Here is the brilliant pearl we found.

The Holy Spirit illuminated us with his charism and showed us that our brother or sister, whom we once regarded as an obstacle, can actually become the very way to God. They actually become an opening, a gateway, a road, a path that leads us to him.

Naturally there is this one condition, that they do not lead us astray with behavior that is on the purely human level. Rather we must engage them with our supernatural behavior. How? You know the answer to that: by loving them. Love them one by one throughout the day, all day long. Love them with that art of loving which is divine, because this can be done only if we have the infused love of the Holy Spirit in our hearts.

We all know what that requires.

What will happen if we do that?

We will be aware of God's presence, for example, in the evening during our prayer, and then also during the day when, for a moment, we can be alone to recollect ourselves before God.

He comes to us, because we have reached out to him in our neighbor.

Many of us experience a union which we do not yet know how to define or categorize, perhaps because it is new. It is a kind of spiritual awareness which fills our hearts with love.

So in his presence we can review our behavior.

One of the results will be that we attained our goal through loving our neighbors. Not only will they be blessed by us, but they become our benefactors, because they have obtained for us what we were seeking all along.

We should be grateful to them. That will give us humility, a virtue most helpful in loving.

Mutual Love

"This is my commandment, that you love one another as I have loved you. No one has greater love than this, to lay down one's life for one's friends."

(John 15:12–13)

Unity: Effect of the Eucharist

True love, the art of loving, reaches its highest point in *loving one another*.

We love one another in such a way that it invites the gift of unity. We are not able to produce it ourselves. Jesus prayed to the Father for unity, but did not command it.

We can do our part by the asceticism of loving one another, but the mystical aspect of unity, the presence of Christ in our midst, must come from heaven.

In our experience, we have seen that unity is the effect of the Eucharist. That is where one becomes truly deified; all are transformed into God (by participation) and become one in him.

The Law of Heaven

The precious pearl, the gem of the gospel is mutual love. Why?

This example will explain it. When an immigrant travels to a distant land, ... he will adapt himself as much as he can to the new environment as he brings his own habits and customs. But he may keep, as much as possible, his own language, his own style of dress and, as often happened in the past, may build a house like those of his own country.

So when the Word of God became man, he adapted himself to this world. He became an infant, a model son, a man, a laborer, but he brought with him the lifestyle of his heavenly homeland. He wanted to establish a new world order for us all, in keeping with the law of heaven, which is mutual love, as the Holy Trinity lives it.

As evidence of this, Jesus said that one commandment was special to him and he called it "my commandment," "a new commandment": "I give you a new commandment, that you love one another. Just as I have loved you, you also should love one another" (Jn 13:34; see also Jn 15:12).

The first Christians who knew Jesus himself or later learned of him, understood this teaching well. In fact, the pagans who observed them said: "See how they love one another and are ready to die for one another."[12]

Jesus referred to this commandment, when he spelled out the measure of mutual love: we must love one another as he has loved us. "Love one another — he said — *as* I love you" (see Jn 15:12).

How has he loved us?

He loved us by giving his life for us.

So, to follow him, we should also be ready to give our life for our brothers and sisters.

What He Asks of Us

We are not always asked to give our life for the others like Jesus did in his total self-offering. But to love our neighbor truly, we must accept those little and great "deaths" which mutual love requires. We must forget ourselves, be detached from things, from our own thoughts and interests, in order to give ourselves completely to the other. We must "make ourselves one" with those who are suffering, and thereby relieve their suffering. We must "make ourselves one" with those who are rejoicing, so their joy will be multiplied.

This is a real dying. "To live for others," "to live the others" implies renunciation of oneself, the spiritual death of the self.

So when we begin to love others in this way and in the process are loved in return, we find ourselves passing from one level of the spiritual life to a higher one; we are aware of a new surge in our interior life.

We experience in a new way the gifts of the Spirit: a joy we never had before, a peace, a benevolence, a generosity.... We find a new way of seeing, which helps us see things as they are before God.

At the same time, this mutual love gives witness of Christ to the world. As Jesus said: "By this everyone will know that you are my disciples, if you have love for one another" (Jn 13:35).

This is the beginning, as we know, of a Christian revolution, a revolution which the first Christians spread all over the known world. As Tertullian said: "We were born yesterday and have invaded the world."[13]

Jesus Did It First

Jesus did not just proclaim the will of God for the "final age." He lived it totally.

He was the first to live total love for God and others, and this is what he asked of others. He did the will of God by giving his life for others.

"No one has greater love than this, to lay down one's life for one's friends" (Jn 15:13). This is the new Law in which we must all walk.

A Heroic Love

What kind of a love is Jesus asking of us?

We know the answer: our love must measure up to the standard Jesus set. It must be a love that is ready to die for others, for each neighbor.

So it must be a heroic love and nothing less. This is love: " … as I have loved you." When love is understood and lived out in that way, it becomes the way to holiness of life.

White Martyrdom

The mutual love which Jesus asks of us is a true martyrdom. In fact he asks of us that we love each other to the point of being ready to die for one another.

We can call this a white (bloodless) martyrdom, if we wish, but it is still a real martyrdom because it asks for our life. It is a daily martyrdom, because we live it moment by moment.

Now in spite of all our good will, we may not have lived that way.

Yet that is the only way we can be true Christians and reach perfection, precisely as martyrs. It will bring us to union with God, to the full presence of Christ in us.

There Is Love and
Then There Is Love

In trying to love God and neighbor I came to realize how we Christians are truly ourselves when we love, that is, when we think not of ourselves but of God and his will. What he wills above all is that we have love for our neighbor.

God wants most of all that we become our true selves. To "fulfill ourselves" as Christians we must "not be," we must live outside ourselves, living as we say "ecstatically." We must live not our own will but the will of God. When we live our neighbor, we are truly ourselves.

I too have tried to live this way, to love. But I realize there is love and then there is love.

I came to see that having some understanding of others and taking a little interest in their sufferings, trying to carry some of their burdens, that is, loving a little here and a little there is not loving as Jesus wants. What God requires of us is real love, loving acts that measure up to his love (at least in our intention and will): "Love one another — he said — as I have loved you" (Jn 13:34).

So we must always be ready to die for our neighbor. Whatever we do moment by moment to show our love concretely must be animated and sustained by this intention, by this decision.

Only that kind of love is pleasing to Jesus. It is not a little bit of love, a veneer of love, but a love so great that we put our life at stake.

In loving this way we live completely "outside ourselves," we entirely renounce ourselves and, when there is more than one of us acting this way, we can hope to renounce ourselves in favor of the risen Lord who can then live in our midst. He is not fully present where there is just a little love, but he is present when we are united in his name, that is, in him, in union with his will, which is to love as he has loved.

Giving One's Life

It is not enough for Christians to be good, merciful, humble, meek, patient.... Christians must have charity for their neighbors.

But — someone may object — don't we have charity if we are good, merciful, patient and forgiving?

No; Christ taught us what charity is. It means that we die for others.

Die. Not just be ready to die, but really die. We die spiritually, renouncing ourselves to "live the others." And even die physically, if necessary.

Charity is not just readiness to give one's life. It is giving one's life.

The Perfection of Love

Saint John, in his first letter, has these beautiful words of encouragement: "If we love one another, God lives in us, and his love is perfected in us" (1 Jn 4:12).

If his love in us is perfect, then we are perfect to the extent that his love in us is perfect.

The perfection of love is found in attaining mutual love.

Reviving Relationships

Just as it is necessary to stir fireplace embers now and then to keep the ashes from smothering the fire, so also is it necessary to make a deliberate effort from time to time to revive mutual love. We must clear away from all our relationships any ashes of indifference, apathy or selfishness.

Nothing But Mutual Love

Let us live mutual love radically, working at it daily, so that we create an atmosphere in which we can declare it always, at every moment.

It would be best if we lived it *as though we had nothing else to do*. Because everything else will take care of itself. Love enhances all our other duties.

So, *think of nothing else*. Think only of promoting mutual love among ourselves. Let us work at *that* all day long. It is absolutely vital for us. By evening we will find ourselves transformed, tired perhaps, but with fresh joy over the wonder of divine life God has set ablaze like fire in our hearts.

Giving Witness

"Love one another." That is the calling of every Christian.

What they said about the early Christians gives us a lot to think about: "See how they love one another and are ready to die for one another."[14]

That means *others were able to see* that each one was ready to die for the other.

Perhaps they saw it in the fact that, in time of persecution, it was not rare for someone to offer his life for someone else. But clearly *they were able to see this* degree of mutual love among Christians.

Today we do not usually face actual dying. Nevertheless, we should be ready to do so. Every act of mutual love implies that we are.

Let us intensify our mutual love. Let every simple smile or gesture directed toward our brothers and sisters, every act of love, every word of appreciation or advice, and every timely correction show our readiness to die for them. We must make our love *visible* not out of vanity but to make sure that we are well-armed and ready to give witness.

We too, like the early Christians, live in a secular world, a world without God. So we must give witness to Jesus and the best way to do this is by our mutual love.

The Dress of a Christian

At times, O Lord, amidst the vanity strolling the city streets, frivolous activities, superficiality, sadness and haste in people everywhere, in every person who passes us by, suddenly the rustle of the habit, the silent and angelic passing of a "little sister of Foucauld," decidedly humble and unassuming, proclaims to our souls the ideal of her founder who shouted the gospel with his life. And in us is reborn more vehemently the desire that we too should "speak you," we too should "shout you."

But how can we, by our own mere passing by, "give you" to the world, "speak you" to the world, be your witnesses, preach you, when we are dressed like everyone else, lost in the crowd as Jesus and Mary were in their times? How will people be able to recognize you?

Once again I feel bubbling up in my heart the gospel response, your solution to our dilemma: "By this everyone will know that you are my disciples, if you have love for one another" (Jn 13:35). This is the attire that ordinary Christians, old and young, men and women, married or not, adults and children, sick or healthy, can wear in order to shout out always and everywhere with their own lives the One they believe in, the One they want to love.

"By This Everyone Will Know ..."

These words always impressed me: "By this everyone will know that you are my disciples, if you have love for one another" (Jn 13:35). "If you have love...." This means if you do not have love in your heart and soul ... then they will not know. How often we are involved in so many things, even good things, but we do it all without love for the person who is right there beside us!

Yet this and this alone is Christianity. This is the revolution that we Christians are to incite.

Unity in Thought

Another effect of living mutual love in a radical way is unity in thought. Mutual love leads from unity of heart to unity of mind.

Being of "one soul" means having the same way of feeling and thinking, which is that of Jesus. If we are incorporated into Christ and are one with him, then having divisions and contrary thoughts would be dividing Christ up.

Mutual love among the first Christians led to oneness of thought; it was not just a counsel but a most urgent plea. Paul wrote: "I appeal to you, brothers and sisters, by the name of our Lord Jesus Christ, that all of you should be in agreement and that there should be no divisions among you, but that you should be united in the same mind and the same purpose" (1 Cor 1:10).

Naturally, this harmony was achieved in those days and still is achieved through communion. It requires a mutual love which brings about the presence of Jesus in our midst (see Mt 18:20).

If there was any danger of disharmony among the first Christians, they were told to let go of their own ideas so that charity could be preserved and there might be oneness of thought among them. Paul wrote to the Romans: "Welcome those who are weak in faith, but not for the purpose of quarrelling over opinions" (Rm 14:1). He did not want any lack of charity to arise from some minor issue or from a different way of reasoning. One of the qualities Paul stresses for mutual charity is tolerance.

The same thing happens today too. Sometimes we may be convinced that a given way of thinking is best, but the Lord suggests to us that if we want to safeguard charity with others, it is better to let go of our own ideas and do what is less perfect in harmony with others than do what is more perfect in discord. This willingness to bend rather than cause division is one of the most efficacious ways of maintaining unity. While it may be difficult, it is blessed by God and accords with the thinking of Christ, who knows its value.

Mutual Love among Christians

The Churches need to love one another too: "May the love with which you loved me be in them — Jesus asked the Father — and I in them" (Jn 17:26).

Unfortunately we have forgotten his testament and our divisions have scandalized the world, the very world to which we are to proclaim him. Churches down through the centuries have remained entrenched in their own doctrinal positions, without any openness or interest in relating to others.

Each of our Churches today needs a fresh supply of love. Christianity itself is in need of a torrent of love.

We need mutual love among the Churches, a love which would lead to putting everything in common, and make each one a gift for the others, so that we can look to a future in which the truth, while remaining one and one alone, can be expressed in various ways, observed from multiple perspectives and enhanced with various theological approaches.

The Risen Lord in Our Midst

"Where two or three are gathered in my name, I am there among them."
(Matthew 18:20)

As we said before, when love measures up to the standard of the new commandment, "Love one another as I have loved you," and we are ready to give our life, then it brings about the presence of the Risen Lord in the midst of the Christian community, which begins to live the life of the Trinity. The art of loving leads us naturally in this direction.

If We Are United Jesus
Is in Our Midst

If we are united, Jesus is among us. And this has value. It is worth more than any other treasure that our heart may possess; more than mother, father, brothers, sisters, children. It is worth more than our house, our work, or our property; more than the works of art in a great city like Rome; more than our business deals; more than nature which surrounds us with flowers and fields, the sea and the stars; more than our own soul.

It is he who, inspiring his saints with his eternal truths, leaves his mark upon every age.

This too is his hour. Not so much the hour of a saint but of him, of *him among us*, of him living in us as we build up — in the unity of love — his Mystical Body.

But we must enlarge Christ, make him grow in other members, become like him bearers of Fire.

Make one of all and in all the One.

It is then that we live the life that he gives us, moment by moment, in charity.

The basic commandment is brotherly love. Everything is of value if it expresses sincere fraternal charity. Nothing we do is of value, if there is not the feeling of love for our brothers and sisters in it. For God is a Father and in his heart he has always and only his children.

The Kingdom of God in Our Midst

Having Jesus in our midst was an over-whelming experience for us!* Perhaps we can never say just *when* he is in our midst, because it presupposes that we are in the state of grace and no one can be certain of being in God's grace. Yet what is certain is that when our common life was based on the sincere resolve to be ready to die for one another as Jesus wants, and all our activity conformed to that — since we must always have "above all, a constant love for one another" (see 1 Pt 4:8) — he very often seemed to make us in simple ways aware of his presence.

So as we felt joy and sorrow, anguish and doubt, on a deeper level the spiritual presence of Jesus among us brought a peace to our souls which was his alone, a fullness of joy which is found only in him, a power and conviction which is not so much the fruit of reason and will, but comes as a special gift from God.

His presence superabundantly rewarded every sacrifice we made and justified every step we took toward him on this path. It put all things and every circumstance in the right light, sooth-ing our sorrows and tempering any excessive joy.

---

* The author recalls here the beginning of the Focolare Movement and the birth of the spirituality of unity.

Every one of us, as we avoided subtle rationalizing and believed in his words with childlike fascination and put them into practice, enjoyed the Kingdom of God in our midst, as a foretaste of paradise for those who are united in his name.

Trinitarian Life

From the earliest days of the Movement we understood that fidelity to mutual love modeled on Jesus crucified and forsaken (that is the *as* in "as I have loved you"*), leads to unity and reflects the life of the Holy Trinity itself.

"Do you know to what extent we should love one another?", we said to ourselves one day before we were familiar with Jesus' testament. We should do it "to the point of being fused into one," just as God, being Love, is three yet one.

This is the very law of heaven which Jesus brought to earth, as I wrote then. We must try to imitate the life of the Holy Trinity, by the grace of God, loving one another as the persons of the Holy Trinity love one another.

The dynamic of this internal life of the Trinity lies in the mutual giving of self, unconditionally. This is eternal and total communion ("All mine are yours, and yours are mine," Jn 17:10).

We see then an analogous reality when God introduces this same lifestyle into human relationships. "I realized — I wrote then — that I am created as gift to the one beside me and the one beside me is created by God as gift to me. Just as the Father in the Trinity is everything for the Son

---

* "This is my commandment: love one another as I have loved you" (Jn 15:12).

and the Son is everything for the Father." And then, "the bond between us is the Holy Spirit, the same bond that unites the persons of the Trinity."

Notes

1   See Saint Augustine, *Homilies on the First Epistle of John*, Homily 5, 7 (Hyde Park, NY: New City Press, 2008), p. 82.

2   F.-R. Chateaubriand, in *Aforismi e citazioni cristiane* (Casale Monteferrato, 1994), p. 17.

3   Erich Fromm, *L'arte d'amare* (Milan, 1971), p. 18.

4   Quoted in Wilhelm Mühs, *Parole del cuore* (Milan, 1996), p. 82.

5   See G. M. Guzzetti, *Islam in preghiera* (Rome, 1991), p. 136.

6   *Mahagga*, 19.

7   See Saint Augustine, *Homilies on the Gospel of John*, Homily 65, 1 (Hyde Park, NY: New City Press, 2010).

8   See Blessed Raimundo da Capua, *Santa Caterina da Siena* (Siena, 1952), pp. 180-181.

9   Quoted in Wilhelm Mühs, *Parole del cuore* (Milan, 1996), p. 82.

10 See Saint Augustine, Sermon 107, in *Sermons* III/4 (Hyde Park, NY: New City Press, 1992).

11 This is a recurring concept in speeches and writings by Igino Giordani (1894-1980).

12 See Tertullian, *Apologia*, 39, 7.

13 See Tertullian, *Apologia*, 37, 7.

14 See Tertullian, *Apologia*, 39, 7.

Sources

(The numbers refer to the page number in the present book, followed by the page number in the cited work by Chiara Lubich.)

English

Essential Writings: Spirituality, Dialogue, Culture (Hyde Park, NY: New City Press, 2008), p. 43: p. 81; p. 62: p. 82; p. 70: pp. 121-122; p. 73: p. 79; p. 92: p. 84; p. 128: p. 84; p. 135: p. 102.

Italian

Cercando le cose di lassù (Rome: Città Nuova Editrice, 1992), p. 36: p. 14; p. 46: pp. 41-42; p. 61: p. 14; p. 94: pp. 44-45; pp. 97-98: pp. 19-20; p. 107: p. 90; p. 108: p. 66; p. 125: pp. 96-97; p. 126: pp. 141-142; p. 127: pp. 137-138.

Costruendo il castello esteriore (Rome: Città Nuova Editrice, 2002), pp. 109-110: pp. 68-69.

Diario 1964/65 (Rome: Città Nuova Editrice, 1985), p. 129: p. 95.

Essere la tua parola (Rome: Città Nuova Editrice, 1980), pp. 47-48: pp. 27-29.

In cammino col Risorto (Rome: Città Nuova Editrice, 1994[4]), p. 59: p. 47-48; p. 123: pp. 41-42.

La vita un viaggio (Rome: Città Nuova Editrice, 1984[4]), p. 40: p. 33; p. 44: pp. 117-118; p. 80: pp. 32-33; p. 83: p. 70; p. 87: p. 63; p. 93: p. 35; p. 119: p. 115; pp. 121-122: pp. 59-60.

L'unità e Gesù abbandonato (Rome: Città Nuova Editrice, 2002[4]), p. 37: pp. 29-30; pp. 81-82: pp. 104-106; p. 86: p. 35; p. 105: pp. 31-32.

Santità di popolo (Rome: Città Nuova Editrice, 2001), p. 88: p. 86; pp. 90-91: p. 74.

Santi insieme (Rome: Città Nuova Editrice, 1984, p. 120: p. 95; p. 124: p. 49.

Scritti spirituali/2 – L'essenziale di oggi (Rome: Città Nuova Editrice, 19972), p. 72: p. 187; p. 104: p. 204.

Scritti spirituali/3 –Tutti uno (Rome: Città Nuova Editrice, 19963), p. 96: p. 82.

Scritti spirituali/4 – Dio è vicino (Rome: Città Nuova Editrice, 19952), p. 58: pp. 209-210; p. 104: p. 204; p. 118: p. 227.

Una via nuova (Rome: Città Nuova Editrice, 2002), pp. 138-139: pp. 42-43.

All other selections come from unpublished writings and are part of the archives of the Chiara Lubich Center, via della Madonella 10, 00040 Rocca di Papa, Rome, Italy.

NEW CITY PRESS
of the Focolare
Hyde Park, New York

New City Press is one of more than 20 publishing houses sponsored by the Focolare, a movement founded by Chiara Lubich to help bring about the realization of Jesus' prayer: "That all may be one" (John 17:21). In view of that goal, New City Press publishes books and resources that enrich the lives of people and help all to strive toward the unity of the entire human family. We are a member of the Association of Catholic Publishers.

Further Reading

The Sun That Daily Rises
Chiara Lubich   ISBN: 978-1-56548-552-5 $6.95
Digitial editions (Kindle, EPUB, PDF) $2.95

His Mass And Ours - Meditations On Living Eucharistically
Brendan Leahy   ISBN: 978-1-56548-448-1 $7.95

The Mystery Of The Eucharist -Voices From The Saints And Mystics
Dennis J. Billy   ISBN: 978-1-56548-530-3 $24.95

The Beauty Of The Eucharist - Voices From The Church Fathers
Dennis Billy   ISBN: 978-1-56548-328-6 $17.95

Periodicals
Living City Magazine,
www.livingcitymagazine.com

Scan to join our mailing list for discounts and promotions or go to www.newcitypress.com and click on "join our email list."